EARLY SIGNS

AF254349

QABAS

Volume 1

By

IFRA'AH

Qabas Volume 1 – Early Signs
By Ifra'ah
Published by Ras al Haq Publications
Copyright 2020 © Ras al Haq Publications
Published in the year 1441 AH/2020 CA
www.irfaa.ca
www.irfaa.ca/rasalhaq

All rights reserved. No portion of this book may be
reproduced in any form or by any means, electronic
or mechanical, including photocopying, recording,
or by any information storage and retrieval system,
without written permission from the publisher.

Cover – original painting by Niaz Kausar

RAS AL HAQ
PUBLICATIONS

Dedicated to

Mohammed Zahir bin Zainul Abideen

my father

Contents

Introduction

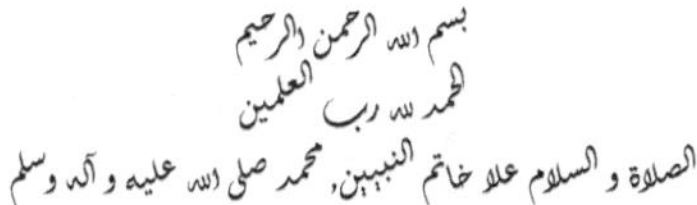

Bism Allah al-Rahman al-Raheem, wa al-hamdu lillahi rabbi al-

alameen, wa 'salaatu wa 'salaamu ala khatamin 'nabiyeen,

Muhammed, sallalaahu alaihi a'lihi wasallam.

In the name of Allah, the love-mercy giving, the eternally loving-

merciful, and all praise and all thanks are to the Lord of all the

universes and all that is in them, and blessings and salutations

upon the seal and completion of the prophets, Muhammed,

greetings of Allah upon him and peace.

This book, the first in a series titled 'Qabas', is dear to my heart as it collects together various pieces written during a period when my old world was falling away and I was being made aware that a new beginning was unfolding, a new life, and my life's calling was becoming apparent. Signs of the calling were with me since birth, but they came to the fore during this period. Hence, I have called this volume - volume 1 - 'Early Signs'. They are pieces written before I began my training under my guide and mentor, Imam Fode Drame of the Jahanke scholars of West Africa who possess an 11 century recorded history as masters of Islamic spirituality and classical scholarship.

The title to the series 'Qabas', was gifted to me via a beautiful vision that I experienced toward the end of my 'suluk', which means the journey or training with one's guide. I will attempt to share it here, but my words will be a poor description, that nevertheless I hope will allow you to have a glimpse or taste of it;

[The Qabas Vision

As I was seated in remembrance and contemplation one night, in front of me appeared a great stag, shining and shimmering in whiteness, and there was a concentration of brilliant white light above its head. The stag was some feet away and was moving toward me. As it got closer, I could see that the white light on its head was emanating from a flaming brand, a torch, lit, glowing with brilliant white star-like light. The flaming brand, 'qabas' in Quranic Arabic, was as if a projection from the top of its head. The stag came straight toward me, approached me until it was so near I could have reached out and touched it, and then the flaming brand that was on its head, was suddenly but so naturally, held by it in its mouth. The stag bowed its head and placed this flaming brand, this qabas at my feet, and disappeared. As this happened the following verse flashed through my mind, and I knew I had been given permission to spread the teachings that are coming to me, and I was given the name under which to do so; It is 'Qabas', a flaming brand.

إِذْ رَأَى نَارًا فَقَالَ لِأَهْلِهِ امْكُثُوا إِنِّي آنَسْتُ نَارًا لَعَلِّي آتِيكُم مِّنْهَا بِقَبَسٍ أَوْ أَجِدُ عَلَى النَّارِ هُدًى

Quran: surah 20, ayah 10

When he saw a fire he said to his family, "tarry here, I have indeed perceived a fire maybe I can bring you from it a flaming brand or I can find guidance at the fire"

The above verse appears in the 20th chapter of the Quran, which is titled 'ta-ha' after the two mystical letters (letters whose meaning we don't know) that make its first sign. [A quranic verse is called 'ayah' in Arabic. 'ayah' means 'sign' and as each sentence in the Quran is considered a cosmic sign, they are never called verses, but always signs]. The context of the verse is that the prophet Moses (peace be upon him) was traveling through the desert with his family. Cold and weary, it must have been nighttime and perhaps they were somewhat lost. Moses (peace be upon him) perceives a fire and says to his family he will go to bring from it a 'qabas' a flaming brand, a torch for warmth and a light for guidance. As the narrative continues, Moses (peace be upon him) does approach the sacred fire, and there has his first encounter with the Divine. And thus, we understand that the qabas he sought to bring was to be one lit by a Divine light.

The word 'qabas' appears once more in the Quran, again in the same context;

إِذْ قَالَ مُوسَى لِأَهْلِهِ إِنِّي آنَسْتُ نَارًا سَآتِيكُم مِّنْهَا بِخَبَرٍ أَوْ آتِيكُم بِشِهَابٍ قَبَسٍ لَّعَلَّكُمْ تَصْطَلُونَ

Quran: surah 27, ayah 7

When Moses said to his family, " I have indeed perceived a fire and I will soon bring you from it news [about the way] or I will bring you a blazing flaming brand so that perhaps you may warm yourselves"

Here the word qabas is further enhanced by the adjective 'shihaabin' meaning 'blazing, luminous, comet, star-like'.

Thus we are honoured indeed to be given such a title for these works. God willing we will continue to publish them under the series title 'Qabas'. The first four volumes of which will be poetry, of which many in later volumes, are didactic. We pray that the One Divine blesses them to truly be a qabas for all travelers and seekers, those who are looking for warmth and guidance upon the way, and may it be so for them, lit from a Divine light.]

This volume, 'Early Signs' is arranged such that it totals 40 pieces, with 10 each being under the four categories of; 'tawheed' or Divine oneness, 'the beloved' referring to the messenger Muhammed (peace be upon him) who is given the title 'the beloved', love, and du'a or prayer. In Islamic tradition we understand the number 40 to carry blessings, and blessed are collections made of 40. We also consider 40 to be the year of second birth or when a person reaches their true adulthood and thus their true life. So it is fitting then, that we begin to publish these volumes in what is the 40th year of my life, a time I never expected to reach. And a time, indeed where I find myself in a new life.

Volumes 2 and 3 are arranged so that they have 64 pieces each. 64 being an elevation of 4 to the third power. A number and organization of numbers that plays a profound role in living matter via DNA as biologists are familiar with; DNA being based on a 4 base pairing whose code is in turn read based on a triplet signage (each set of three DNA bases forming one amino acid code or 'codon'). Volume 4 is composed of 47 pieces written during the end stage of my suluk. Volumes 2, 3 and 4 are thus writings during my journey and take a more didactic flavor. God willing we will elaborate on them in the introductions to the volumes in which they are published.

Volume 5 (to be printed, tentatively titled 'The book of names') and those after, are writings after the completion of my journey and have begun my life's work as a teacher of Islamic spirituality.

To end, I pray that the simple words in this volume and those in volumes to come God willing, will be a source of Divine light giving guidance, and Divine love, a warmth that comforts strengthens and quickens you on the way, so you may reach home safe and sound, and may I meet you there.

-Ifra'ah

24th Ramadan 1440.

Canada.

Ackowledgements

I especially want to thank Niaz Kausar, the artist who so patiently listened to my rendition of the vision, and who translated that into the amazing cover design of this book. Painting over the course of many months, and enrolling the help of many others. All of them volunteering their time and effort. My heartfelt thanks to you all. I am amazed by such gifts freely given. I also want to thank my many friends all around the world, who have sheltered, fed, driven around, hosted and assisted me in so many ways over the past months that I have been a nomad on the path. And my thanks to my dear students and friends who have helped with proofing this work.

My thanks of course to my teacher, guide and mentor, Imam Fode Drame, who told me so many years ago that I must publish this work. He has brought me safely to my journey's end and continues to be a light and inspiration, a strength and a mentor.

May the One Divine bless and protect, nourish and strengthen, and elevate you all in this world and in the eternal existence to come.

Finally, my thanks to my grandmother, Um Razeena bint Qasim, who is as my soul.

TAWHEED

An ocean wooing a raindrop

An ocean wooing a raindrop,
That came from that same ocean.
But somewhere in the clouds,
Forgot where it came from.

The water must return,
And every river flow to the sea.
For the ocean to call the drop,
It is not necessary.

Yet it does, ceaselessly.
Mighty roar and gentle lapping,
Echoed within each detached particle,
Hydrogen and oxygen colliding.

An ocean wooing a raindrop,
That came from that same ocean,
The water is returning.

∞

Bearing witness

By the unlettered word,
that flows through me.

By the blinding light,
That is the break of day.

By the birds that soar over the ocean waves,
And the whales flocking below.

By the water that gives life,
And the stars that birth planets.

By the meteors that streak,
And are kept out by angel-shields.

By the full moon at night,
I bear witness that I am a single self

Created by the Unlimited One
*Al Ahad**!

And I bear witness
that I am on my way

Back to The One
Back to home.

*Al Ahad is a name of The One Divine that means The One. The Oneness of the Divine is an all-encompassing reality, where nothing is devoid of Divine presence, whether known or unknown, acknowledged or un-acknowledged, the One Divine is in, and controls all, and, everything. All else is paired, except the One, and hence The One, is the only true Divine.

Glory to The One who created all in pairs, in what is from the earth, and in themselves, and in what they do not know. (Quran 36;36)

سُبْحَانَ الَّذِي خَلَقَ الْأَزْوَاجَ كُلَّهَا مِمَّا تُنبِتُ الْأَرْضُ وَمِنْ أَنفُسِهِمْ وَمِمَّا لَا يَعْلَمُونَ

subahaana-lladhi khalaqal-azwaaja kullaha mimma thunbithul-ardhu wa min anfusihim wa mimma la ya'alamoon.

∞

Learning to be

Learning to be,
Not taking.
My blood flows through me,
Unblocked.
The sun shines through me.
From north to south,
East to west.
I am only a glass prism,
Reflecting diving light.

Cleared up of pent-up fear,
Should the storms come,
Should people hate me,
Injure or attack.
Should the earth shake from under my feet,
I will not fear.
Glass will only be clarified.
Impurities further purged.
By white-hot fire.

Shining like a light-house beacon,

To all who come,
Or do not.
Reflecting light.
Love of Allah the flame of my heart,
Manifested bright.
To all apparent,
By my will, my glad acquiescence.
Surrender is my glory.

∞

Manifest promise

From the great bear rainforest
to the tracts of the Sahara
From the Cape of Good Hope
to Greenland's ice-fields
Continents, and the clouds that
fly over the oceans
Eagles soar and Dolphins sonar
Giraffes their tall necks sway
in graceful arcs moving as they run
Dwarfing the trees. And whale pods roam
Racing the currents and tumbling in between
deep and ocean swell
While ants build nests
and people walk to work
Cultivate in remote places
And consume in loud cities
Civilizations are dug up by archeologists
Who fight over rights to some bust
of some dead person.
This earth turns.
Matter dies, rots and becomes trees again

And again and again.
But a soul. A single soul
Leaves this earth for eternity.

Standing on the top of Mt. Everest
I behold the earth below me. I touch the sky
And do not deny.
Do not deny my continuation.
My Lord I worship Thee.
A prayer for my existence.
One. Almighty.

I do not deny my return to Thee
The eternity promised to me.

∞

My home calls me

My home calls me,
In whispered breath that escapes
When a blade of grass is bent
By some unknowing child's caressing hand
Eager to pick the dandelion flower
And blow away those petals
On the arms of a waiting wind.

My home calls me,
In tears that lace my lower eyelid
Not sufficient to flow-out and wet
A cheek bathed in soft moonlight
As I stare at distant planets
Visible as drops of piercing light
Retina welcomes the transcendent visitor.

My home calls me,
In that knowing gleam in the eye
Of the lone stork that came to sit
On top of the weeping willow
By the shores of the small hidden pond

In a park by the ocean where
I went to walk to soothe my aching heart.

        My home calls me,
And O my Lord, you are my only witness
How gloriously rich to have
My home's master
Be my constant Guide and closest Confidant
It eases this parting and I am joyful
Knowing I would not be here except You
willed it so.

Ah, but my home calls me,
And its call cannot be drowned out but
By the mirthful chatter
of tedious fleeting pleasures.

If you love these pleasures, beware,
they may drown the call out completely.
And if you are impatient at strife, be grateful,
for pain that will allow you to see.

        So happy then,
are the days Balanced between
summer rain and winter sun
Happy to live, and living not forget.

That happier home
to which I am every day
Drawing closer.

O my Lord, grant Thou me,
A joyous homecoming
and a splendid reunion.

∞

Signs

*Ayaath**, signs,
Envelope me
Stars and planets, earth and sky
Every drop in every river
flows to meet the sea.
Every cell in every body
Pulsates to an internal decree.

DNA is mathematical wonder
Encoding life caught in a seed
Dormant, till moist earth feeds
So arises from the dead molecular
an alive quantum state.
The seed is now a fragrant flower.

Music is number in motion
*Dhikr*** on the tongue resonates
With a chorus continuous sung
        in angel-realm

Truths equate, bringing into vibration,
Heartstrings stubbornly silent
Woken to heavenly joy,
     remembering whence it came.

Like that unrelenting flow to the ocean,
All knowledge spirals upward, upward
We are risen, a disciple caught
in the current source-bound
to everlasting home.
     You to your Creator.
Me to the same.
     Each one to The One***.

These revealed words of God, *ayaath*
of metaphysical beauty,
     serenade the soul,
vaporize stains so heart-pores can open.
And a seed grows, its water met.
Like that tree, head
     buried to the ground
In a life-long prostration.
     You grow tall.

A wonder to behold, a canopy,
        a nesting place and a shade
Between the two books of signs
Barriers break down and they merge
Each shining upon the other
The slave surrenders in
        bewildered wonder
And tajweed sounds carry
        the heart back to its maker

Marrying the external to the internal
ayaath of creation to *ayaath* of revelation
To open the *ayaath* in the soul
        to remember
That place called home and recalibrate
The course of this traveler, and replenish
Provision for this wayfarer

From within and without
From sound and touch and beyond the
        five-senses
To where the soul feels, from every
        quantum universe
A proclamation reverberates
God is One, God is One, God is One.

You are a living proof that cannot escape
One day I will join you,
our streams joining to meet the ocean
You and me and all that exists and ever
      did exist, and ever will
All to Allah. Time transcended
Before The Creator, realization
Signs brought to final fruition.

∞

When I stop conforming,
And let everything be.
clarity, what clarity.

Knowing then who I am,
My origin and my end,
I know me, I know me.

O' then, immense joy,
Explodes, spreads and permeates,
Every part of me.

Connection cemented,
Light upon light I become.
Surrendered to Unity.

∞

Trust

Taught to trust, through hours
When my feet swell and my body sways

In imperceptible waves deeper into submission
Gently the rhythm of the recitation

Draws me in, winds down the
    deception of ego
Until there is nothing left, but
    my primordial state

Standing before my Lord in my *fitri*-self*
Is bliss. I breathe peacefully suspended
In this place of love, ensconced.

Rising and falling, as my breaths
Join to the rhythm of the Universe

This reverberation
Ramadan night resonation
For a moment, split second divine

Time resets and the heart is rebirthed

The soul's polish reaches that first sparkle
When polishing cloth leaves the surface

And before dust settles
Momentary opening
to light upon light.

Nanosecond reflection of that
    originating light
So weighty, yet so ethereally weightless

So substantial, everywhere, yet no where
It explodes-in, quiet, as it if was always there

It radiates from a point,
yet seems to be everywhere at once

A long night to clean the mirror
    that is my soul
And I, polished-mirror-soul

Reflecting this *nur***,
till I am nothing
In a sea of light
Then I find trust

Implicit, immaculate, perfect, absolute

I am slave
And my Lord looks after me

*fitra is the natural disposition. (fitri-self explains this natural self). It means the state of being of all of creation, i.e., their natural state. The natural state of all of creation is to be in devotion the One Divine. That is, all creation is in a constant state of worshipping or glorifying the One Divine. The human body is also doing this all the time. But the human faculty of consciousness has been given the freedom to chose to join the body (and the rest of creation) or not. That is, the human has the faculty of free choice. When the human chooses to return to the natural state, that is, to join the rest of creation, and also join the consciousness to the human body, and be in a state of worship, then peace and completion enters. This is the meaning of Islam. We know that all of creation is a constant state of worship from the numerous statements in the Quran, such as the one below.

All in the heavens and in the earth are in glorification of Allah, The Sovereign, The Pure, The Noble, The Wise (Quran62:1)

يُسَبِّحُ لِلَّهِ مَا فِي السَّمَاوَاتِ وَمَا فِي الْأَرْضِ الْمَلِكِ الْقُدُّوسِ الْعَزِيزِ الْحَكِيمِ

yusabbihu lillahi wa fi-ssamawathi wa ma fi-lardhil-malikil-quddusil-a'zeezil-hakeem.

***nur is Divine Light, that shines through every creation (alive or dead) that is in a state of fitra- or it's natural disposition, which is to be a devotee of the One Divine*

∞

When time breaks down

My faith reverberates through the Universe
Every sunflower that follows the sun,
Every bee that hums
All the raindrops caught on a spider's web

Proclaim God is Great!
And there is only One.

Between Creator and created

As endless as the winds that cover this planet
As deep as the sleep of the dead
As irresistible as the rocks turning
to desert sand
Is the bond between Creator and created.

We will return

Every soul return,
Every 'one' returning to The One.

When time breaks down.

∞

Al- Qayyum

Light follows darkness
And day follows night
Ease follows hardship
And there is sweetness in grief
The slave has lost herself
and come to the Master
In depravity, needing peels away
The veil of ego
So as to know
The slave is not the possessor
of self-sufficiency
The Master is alone *Al-Qayyum**

**Al Qayyum is one of the Asma Allah, the most beautiful names of the One Divine. It means the one who is self-sufficient and by whom all things subsist.*

∞

THE BELOVED

peace be upon him

He who acceded (ascension)

From your reverie-sleep
You were woken*.
After loss upon loss, deep depravation
You father-figure taken, then your beloved
Who was your strength,
when you doubted yourself.

Afraid of insanity, she put peace in your heart
your solace and right hand,
the first who believed in your mission
and your garment against
the rain
Of brutality to come.

Then humiliation on hurt.
Showered as stones hurled by children, goaded
to hate.
Caused your sensitive heart to bleed, yet your
breast
as wide as the universe you did not falter.

Did not hate, did not complain except
to the One
who loves to hear complaints.
*"as long as you are not displeased with me My Lord, I
am happy"*

Ah, *Ahmed**, the chosen one,
the praised one
The one for whom the universe sings praise
The stars sigh, the oceans cry,
and every leaf on every tree,
longs to wear green in your honour.

the moon weeps seeing your beauty,
and the sun rejoices to cast its rays
upon your strong back,
held upright as you walk
in paced strides that cause
the earth to glorify her maker
that your feet touch her.

And that your sleep is now in her.
And the realm of the angels
joins the Almighty God
Who He himself, Glorious and exalted!
Sings your praises^*

So all of creation praises you and I praise you.
O *Muhammed**, what a creation!
O God send your blessings upon your beloved!

From your reverie-sleep by the *ka'ba**.
Resting there in that sanctity
The house of God, inviolable.
Your choice a testimony of trust.

Constant state of the greatest of human hearts
as wide as the universe.
A heart in complete trust,
in *Al-Rahman**. Immaculate.
Absolute.
Not an atom of doubt to mar
purity of worship
Your secret of secrets. True felicity.

Trust reciprocated, you were woken
by the angel,
Peace be upon the most noble emissary
Who summoned you,
to the furthest mosque*.
Jerusalem. There you lead the whole host of
the prophets of God*
In a *salat** that must have shook the earth to its
molten core

The *sujood*-force* of the hundreds of thousands
of august foreheads
Pressed to the earth.
What ranks upon ranks!

Standing, bowing, sitting, prostrating
And the voice of the *imam**, your voice,
O beloved of God
That voice, that all the birds
for all time get their sweetness from,
that *ru'ku**, the gaze of which must
have fertilized the earth till the end of time.

Then you, a great sun among a galaxy of stars
Ascended through heaven upon heaven,
Till all seven were in your memory.
And the gates of where even Gabriel
Upon whom be peace, dared not enter,
Were opened,
For you.

And you did not refuse the call,
O chosen one!
How great is your heart not to refuse,
What it saw.
O beloved of God
How great is your heart not to refuse,

What it saw.

O beloved of God
Your accession is our accession.
You taught. '*the salat is the mi'raj* of the believer*'
A generosity incapable of encapsulation
by the universe
You have given your great gift to us.
O Messenger, Chosen one.

Only Allah *jallajalaaluhu** knows
The extent of His love for you.
O beloved of God.

This needy slave of the One
beyond time and space
Thanks her Lord for your creation
with a thanks eternal.

By every moment in time,
By your great chosen one,
O our beloved Lord, bring us closer to him,
Heal us with the light of Muhammed
The one who acceded.

Sallu ala an-Nabi!

Allahumma salli ala habeebina wasayyidina

wamaulana Muhammed

Praise and salute the prophet!
O Allah send you salutations upon our beloved
and our leader and our master Muhammed, and
upon his blessed family, and his companions,
with a greeting that is compete peace.

The incident referenced here will be given below, and all Arabic terms will be given in alphabetical order after it.

The incident referenced is the 'mi'raj' of the blessed messenger of The One Divine. Mi'raj means ascension. The last messenger, Muhammed, peace be upon him, had undergone the most difficult phase in his mission when the mi'raj took place. The Meccan tribes had placed himself and his followers under cruel sanctions that caused many of them to die of starvation. First, he lost his uncle who was a protector and father-figure to him (he had lost his father before his birth and his mother, when he was six years old), and then his beloved wife of 25 years died. She, whose name is Khadija (and we give her the epithet Al-Kubra, the great one) was the first to believe in his mission when he was called to prophethood ten years previously. She had faith in him when he himself thought he was going insane, as his encounters with The One Divine's word and angels came about. Shortly after losing these two great supports, the sanctions were lifted and Muhammed was allowed to move freely. He went to a nearby town seeking protection and bringing to the people there the message that they must worship the One Divine. He was met by ridicule and the town's elders had the children chase him out by pelting him with stones. This was especially hard to bear. Bruised and bleeding, when he was resting outside the town, The One Divine sent an angel to him asking if he wanted retribution. He replied asking that The One Divine forgive all people in the town, pleading for them that they are do not know what they are doing and saying that perhaps their later generations will believe (a prayer that was granted). And then he asked the One Divine for help, saying that no matter what happened to him, as long as his Maker was not unhappy with him, he didn't mind. He returned to Mecca and sometime after this was reclining one night, resting against the walls of the ka'ba (vide infra). When he was thus resting, the angel Gabriel (peace be upon him) appeared to him and took him on a mystical and miraculous journey. First, they traveled to Jerusalam, which is called 'the furthest mosque', and there all the previous messengers and prophets of the One Divine joined Muhammed to perform the salat. Muhammed lead that salat as the imam. After this, Gabriel took him and they ascended through the seven heavens up to the door of the Divine presence. Beyond this threshold even Gabriel was not allowed to enter, but Muhammed was given audience, and entered the closest presence with the One Divine. This miraculous journey termed 'isra'a wa al-mi'raj', or the assencion occurred in the space of a moment, transcending the commonly known dimesions of space and time. Muhammed subsequently taught us that every believer is able to experience the same asscesion and closeness with the One Divine, during their salat.

Al-Rahman* is one of the most beautiful
names of the One Divine that means the
gracious tender love.

Ahmed* is the name of the last messenger that
means the one who is praised

imam* is the one who leads the salat, when a
group performs it in synchronization.

jallajalaaluhu* glorious is the majesty of the
One Divine

ka'ba*, literally cube (the English word cube
comes from the Arabic 'ka'ba'). The ka'ba is
a cubical monument dedicated to the worship
of The One Divine, that was first built by
Abraham (peace be upon him) several
thousand years previously, in a barren land
where he had been commanded by the One
Divine to leave his young wife Hajara (peace
be upon her) and their infant son, Isma'eel
(peace be upon him). Hajara persevered and
founded the city of Mecca. Abraham would
visit them and during one of these visits, the
commandment from the One Divine came to
build the ka'ba. The ka'ba exists to this day,

making it the oldest known monument
dedicated to the worship of the One Divine.
All Muslims face it when making the salat.

Mi'raj* — ascension

Muhammed* is a derivation of the name
Ahmed, that means the one whose essence is
praise, or the one continuously in a state of
being praised.

ru'ku* is the act during the salat, where the
palms of the hands are placed on the knees
and the back is bent to parallel the earth, and
the gaze is kept to where the forehead will
touch the earth in sujood. It is a bowing
position.

salat* - the ritual worship performed at a
minimum five times a day by a Muslim. It
means to re-calibrate, re-align or make right.
It is the physical, mental, emotional and
spiritual act that reconnects the human being
with the One Divine.

sujood* is the act during the salat, where the
forehead, nose, palms of the hands, knees,

and toes are placed on the ground in prostration to the One Divine. It is akin to the feotal position.

^ The One Divine's words are referenced;*
Verily, Allah and His angels, do send salutations upon the prophet. O you who have entered belief, send also salutations upon him, and greet him with submitted peace. (Quran 33:56)

إِنَّ اللَّهَ وَمَلَائِكَتَهُ يُصَلُّونَ عَلَى النَّبِيِّ ۚ يَا أَيُّهَا الَّذِينَ آمَنُوا صَلُّوا عَلَيْهِ وَسَلِّمُوا تَسْلِيمًا

Inna-llaha wa malaa'ikathahu yusalloona a'ala-nnabiy, ya ayyuhalladheena a'manu sallu a'laihi wa sallimu tasleema.

∞

Natural state of praising him

A poet is not made but born
A bird does not sing except to voice its song
My heart cannot love but by loving you
O Muhammed,
for whom the moon split*

The river does not flow up but down
A painting can only be when paint is used
There is no meaning in my everyday
Except when it is spent,
Remembering you,
O Muhammed

A pen is not a pen if ink does not flow
My lips do not find their fulfillment
except in smiling
And my eyes theirs, in tearing
Full of love-light, praising you,
O Muhammed

The log that was parted from your step
Heaved sobs that shook the universe
Heaved sighs
as if its bark was being ripped open**
And so my chest hurts in ceaseless ache, missing
you,
O' Muhammed

*among the signs signaling the birth of the
final messenger of the One Divine, was that
the moon split on the night of his birth, and
then rejoined. Many witnessed this.
** when the final messenger was preaching,
he used to stand on an old log. Later, a lady
had made for him a pulpit. When it was
delivered and he was about to climb the
pulpit to deliver a sermon, the old log, now
kept in a corner emitted a loud and heart-
breaking sob, that was heard by all present.
All creation, animate and inanimate,
recognize and love the final messenger, and
so this old log was heartbroken that it would
no longer be what the prophet would stand
upon. Muhammed (peace be upon him),
when he heard this, immediately descended

*the pulpit and went and hugged the log to
console it.*

∞

O my Lord send peace and blessings upon

your beloved

Maula ya salli wa sallim ala Muhammed

'O my Lord send peace and blessings upon your
beloved
The best and perfect of creation that you've created'

Ramadan approaches,
and I remember my prophet.
More than ever, he walks with me.
In front of me and I trot,
to keep up with his stride.
So fast and steady,
Going to meet his enemy
Walking upon your work.

'O my Lord send peace and blessings upon your
beloved

The best and perfect of creation that you've created'

Ramadan is nigh,
and I remember my prophet.
His hand is on my head,
and all my pain has disappeared.
I close my eyes and a great peace,
enters my heart.
As his hand strokes my hair,
I raise my eyes to his kind face,
And everything is alright.

'O my Lord send peace and blessings upon your
beloved
The best and perfect of creation that you've created'

Ramadan is here,
and I remember my prophet
He jokes and gently laughs with me,
in breaks in the long night prayer
His feet swell as the hours pass
and his beard becomes soaked
I follow him in the prayer
and stand with him.

My soul in peace
A great joy in worshiping thee.

How I miss him.

∞

O' patient man

(sallalaahualaihiwasallam)*

Whispers have brought down empires.
Written in human history.

And each day in some mundane home,
Some husband walks out on his wife.
By a neighbor who whispered,
Or on the street a rumour spread.

Brothers do not speak to sisters,
For years. Afraid to allow that,
the human condition will err.
Afraid to forgive lest it may,
reduce their honour or display,
their heart's fragility.

The devils can only whisper.
Our only enemy. Recall,
Abu Sufyan**. Foe that turned
to the friend of Islam. And that
great stalwart of the deen***, who first
tried to kill the blessed prophet.

O patient man! Teach us your patience.
Your people are in disarray,
They kill each other, deceived,
By the chief deceiver. They spur,
Ever onto heinous bloodshed.
While screaming 'Allah is greater'

None but a heart serene is safe,
On that day. O didn't you know?
Allah decreed that our father
Ibraheem say, and Ahmed teach
Upon them both be lofty peace
Our sole foe – a doomed whisperer.

Doomed to rot in hell forever.
Will you rot with him, when you can
Be with the blessed beloved?

In that great heaven. For his sake,
Love your brother and purify,
A human heart so fit to gift

To him who loved those who plotted
his murder. To him who showed mercy
to they who martyred his people
He who loved every dog,
and cat and tree. And every
camel called him friend. And plants,
grew at his touch in glee. Children,
played around his feet, freely kissed
By the greatest man among men.
And woman flocked, confident they,
would find a kindred confidante.
A guiding light who understood.

Then love your brother, if you would
truly believe, love for them what
You love for yourself. So taught us,
Muhammed, chosen messenger.
All heavy burdens fall away,
From weary shoulders when they,
Surrender. And forehead on ground,
heart is freed to expand and fly.

Upwards on a gentle breeze like,
a feather guided to heaven.

The cursed whisperer vanquished.
Muhammed's light will guide you home,
Sallalaahu alaihi wasallam*

*sallalaahu alaihi wasallam — Salutations of the One Divine be upon him and the Divine greeting.

**Abu Sufyan was the leader of the enemies of Muhammed, who lead armies against Muhammed and his followers. He later became a Muslim.

***Omar (God be pleased with him) first tried to kill the beloved messenger, and became his ardent follower during his attempt to do so. He went on to become of the greatest followers of Muhammed (peace be upon him).

∞

The moon outshines the stars

The moon outshines the stars,
And the sun outshines them all.
I stay awake at night.

And in the day, I am bathed,
by light upon light.
In the night am enveloped,
By cool breezes of mercy.

Closeness with my beloved,
And by him to The Beloved.
Fills my heart and all other pales,
As it should.

For 'truth stands clear from error'
and 'whoever has grasped the handhold of God,
Knows that it will never break'*

The moon has guided my night to daybreak.

*The statement from the One Divine is referenced.

There is no compulsion in the way/religion, Now the right way has become clear from the wrong/truth stands clear from error, whoever rejects the false diety and believes in Allah, so has taken hold of the most trustworthy handhold that has no breaks/weaknesses in it. And Allah is The Hearing, The Knowing' (Quran 2:256)

لَا إِكْرَاهَ فِي الدِّينِ قَد تَّبَيَّنَ الرُّشْدُ مِنَ الْغَيِّ فَمَن يَكْفُرْ بِالطَّاغُوتِ وَيُؤْمِن بِاللَّهِ فَقَدِ اسْتَمْسَكَ بِالْعُرْوَةِ الْوُثْقَىٰ لَا انفِصَامَ لَهَا وَاللَّهُ سَمِيعٌ عَلِيمٌ

laa ikra-aha fee-ddeen, qad thabayyana-rrushdu min-alghaiy, faman yakfur bi-ttaghuthi wayu'min billahi faqadis-thamsaka bil-u'rwathil-wusqaa la-nfisaama laha, wa-llahu samee'un a'leem.

∞

The moon

A twinge of jealousy tonight
I felt, on beholding the moon.
O' moon, full faced and bright!
'As thou dost worship God, so do I'*
I quote my beloved, Allah elevate him!
As he taught, to pray on your sight.

So I gaze on your face enchanted,
With wonder and delight.
And feel my own loss, O' dear Moon,
You saw the prophet's blessed face.
Subhahanallah**! Princely state of grace,
O' I wish I were thee, for that same felicity.

**how Muhammed peace be upon him would
address the moon.*
***Glory be to The One Divine*

∞

Ahmed, the praised one

Ahmed, 'the praised one'
His coming foretold, through the ages.
The seal of the messengers,
All of them honorable.
And he of them the foremost.
O Allah! Send your blessing upon them all

He is the paraclete, comforter.
Soothing world's wounds with mercy.
Dispelling doubt with guidance.
His way is the middle way.
His colour green. The midpoint
of the rainbow spectrum. Between Moses's
earth-violet commandments, and Jesus's
love-red pure aspirations.
O Allah! Send your blessing upon them both

His guidance balanced.
teaching how to live in the world,

And yet be always other-worldly.
His guidance, a center
that yet spans east, west, north and south
All of humanity is chosen for his following*
And may they follow him!

Over traditions, tongues, empires.
Those who chose his way find peace.
Named by divine decree as
Ahmed, 'the one who is praised'
His soul the first created
to be prophet last sent**.

The final messenger. '*Muhammed*'
'He who is excessively
ceaselessly lovingly praised'.
Allah the One, the Only
Called him, 'His beloved'!
Ahmed, Habeebullah

A title reserved only for this
Son of 'God's slave' - *Abdullah*
Son of 'her of verity'- *Amina, noble lady*
Muhammed…Ahmed…Ahmed…

The words linger, drawn on
a longing cry emanating from
the heart of this follower.
Who longs to meet the master,
To once cast her gaze upon
Allah's chosen beloved!

What sorrow or hardship
could afflict a heart that beheld
the beloved of Allah?
the light that is the light of Muhammed,
illuminates the heavens and all the worlds.
For all time, without end
He is praised. Muhammed, the chosen.

> **While all previous messengers were for a time or a people, the last messenger is for all time and all creation, as all are enfolded by One Divine's chosen sent mercy.*
>
> ***Though Adam peace be upon him was the first human being whose clay was fashioned, the soul of Muhammed peace be upon him, was already decreed and made as the final messenger. This is understood from the*

narration recorded from the beloved, peace be upon him;

"Truly I was [already], in the sight of Allah, the Seal of Prophets, when Adam was still kneaded in his clay. I shall inform you of the meaning of this. It is the supplication of my father Ibrahim (Q 2:129) and the glad tidings of my brother ʿIsa to his people (Q 61:6); and the vision my mother saw the night I was delivered: she saw a light that lit the palaces of Syro-Palestine so that she could see them."

(Narrated by Ahmed in the Musnad al-Shamiyyin and elsewhere)

The Quranic verses referenced by the beloved peace be upon him are as follows;

> Our Lord, send among them a messenger from them, who will explain to them your signs and teach them your book and the wisdom and will purify them. Verily You are The Noble, The Wise. (Quran 2:129)

رَبَّنَا وَابْعَثْ فِيهِمْ رَسُولًا مِّنْهُمْ يَتْلُو عَلَيْهِمْ آيَاتِكَ وَيُعَلِّمُهُمُ الْكِتَابَ وَالْحِكْمَةَ وَيُزَكِّيهِمْ ۚ إِنَّكَ أَنتَ الْعَزِيزُ الْحَكِيمُ

Rabbana wab-a'st feehim rasoolan minhum yathlu a'laihim ayaathika wa yu'allimuhumul-kitaba wa-lhikmatha wa yuzakkihim, innaka anthal-azeezul-hakeem.

And when Jesus the son of Mary said, O' people of Israel, verily I am a messenger from Allah to you, confirming the truth of what you have between your hands from the Torah and bringing good news of a messenger who will come after me, his name is Ahmed. And so when he brought to them clear teaching, they said this is magic obviously. (Quran 61:6)

وَإِذْ قَالَ عِيسَى ابْنُ مَرْيَمَ يَا بَنِي إِسْرَائِيلَ إِنِّي رَسُولُ اللَّهِ إِلَيْكُم مُّصَدِّقًا لِّمَا بَيْنَ يَدَيَّ مِنَ التَّوْرَاةِ وَمُبَشِّرًا بِرَسُولٍ يَأْتِي مِن بَعْدِي اسْمُهُ أَحْمَدُ ۖ فَلَمَّا جَاءَهُم بِالْبَيِّنَاتِ قَالُوا هَٰذَا سِحْرٌ مُّبِينٌ

Wa idha qala I'sa ibnu-Maryama ya bane isra-eela inni rasoolu-Allahi ilaikum musaddiqan lima baina yadayya min-thawraathi wa mubashshiran birasoolin ya'thee min ba'adi, ismuhu Ahmed, falamma jaa'ahum bilbaiyyinathi qalu hadha sihrun Mubeen.

∞

The scent from his beard

(sallalaahu alaihi wasallam*)

O Muhammed,
   the scent from your beard**,
   tells me the fragrance of your footsteps,
   That walked to change a globe.

Sent by Allah,
   you were chosen before you arrived.
   And realization of that is opening
   the gates of my soul further into *tawheed****

*Ya mustafa, Ya rauf, Ya raheem*****
   Grant, O our Generous Lord who
   gifted us this greatest of gifts,
   Grant our eternal nearness to him

*Sallalaahu alahi wasallam**

     **vide supra, Salutations of the One Divine
     be upon him and the Divine greeting.*

*** Hairs from the beard of the last
messenger, peace be upon him, emanate a
divine fragrance, which those fortunate
enough to have been in the presence of rare
preserved hairs still extant, treasured in the
Muslim world, have smelled.*

*****tawheed is the realization of Divine
Oneness. It is understood, then tasted,
experience and known.*

******* Ya mustafa, Ya rauf, Ya raheem. 'ya'
is the Arabic for 'O' in address. mustafa,
rauf and Raheem are among the over 250
known titles for the beloved, peace be upon
him. 'Mustafa' means the chosen one.
'Rauf' means kindness. 'Raheem' means the
one showing tender loving mercy.*

∞

Your name is a healing

Your name is a healing,
And your station is praise.
Some say, had it not been for your soul,
The universe wouldn't have been made.

I dedicated my life,
To studying DNA, spent eons,
In mesmerized wonder.
At the greatness of God.
Unraveling just one molecule among millions

Thereby I caught a trace,
Of God's true greatness.
And now my heart and soul and mind are lost
In wonderment at your immense station.

You, whom God called,
His Beloved. His special servant.

O great Creator, your minutest creation,
Is beyond what we can ever understand.

Despite concerted effort,
By the brightest humankind.
Then what must be the state of this man,
Whom You and Your angels
shower blessing upon.

My mind shuts in defeated daze.
And my heart I open,
It is only the human heart
which may comprehend,
That place of love for the chosen one.

Your name is a healing,
my master and my guide.
Some say, had it not been for your soul,
The universe would not have been made.

∞

A sign of the extent of Allah's love

The tears of all of creation,
Has gathered in the oceans.

Since the day you passed into where, you
are closer to your Lord than you are to us.

Ah, but you were always so.
And so these are tears of joy.

That our Lord decreed the making
Of you. O' tremendous soul!

O' one whose station is praise
It was a name decreed.

Chosen for you, O' chosen one!
Before time was brought into existence
Your name was known.

You are the darkness that dissipates the nights
Of confusion. You are the voice of reason.

That yet sings in the highest echelons of love.
You are the middle way.

Yet your way is the most exalted to God,
You are the beloved, and yet loving God,

Completely, you loved all of us deeply,
With a sincerity no human had known before

Or has known since. Or can know.
O' Muhammed! Who after you, can love us

The way you do? O Muhammed
To whom all of creation will run screaming for
help*

O' the one who says '*Ana lahu***'
O' Muhammed, love for you is polish upon the
heart.

Love for you is protection and embellishment
Love for you is adornment with the fragrance

of the highest heaven, where you went.
Not even the mighty beloved Gabriel, upon
whom be lofty peace

Could enter into that station whose fragrance
you emanate. Returning

To show us that Allah loves us
enough to permit your presence among
us. Knowing you, we realize

The full extent of God's love for us
That He decreed that the best of creation
Be you. And you for us.

O' Allah elevate and send your blessing upon
our beloved. Your beloved
The best of creation you have created.
Forever and always, by as much as only You
know the extent of all that exists.

*on the day of judgement, all humankind will
run to Muhammed peace be upon him, asking
him for help.
** he will reply 'ana lahu', 'I am for it!' and
make a prostration to the One Divine, the like
of which has never been known.

∞

THE LOVE

Al Wakeel*

Tears squeezed from eyes too tired to cry,
Cleanse the heart of dirt deeply sewn,
Into every sinew even the heart's owner,
Did not know the when and how.
Of its detested insidious accumulation.

Rebellion, hurt, pain, ocean-deep needs unmet
And loss upon loss upon loss, suffered over years
The slave did not turn to her Maker and so was
                                                soiled
An emptiness filled by deception so she could forget
Her need for return.

The wounded did not know that,
peace and healing and light upon light upon light.
That LOVE, the kind that has no end and no limit
Was just a *mukhraj*** away
Say 'Allaah', touch the roof of your mouth and
                                                breathe

Deeply breathe.
Had I known this, maybe I would not have
                              soiled myself
In vainly seeking for my help in myself,
Or in others or in rebellion or in indulgences
                              that only
Bring the devils closer and closer to me.

And an ego grew that knew no bounds and
Relied only on itself.
And now, eyes too tired to squeeze out tears.
Pain upon pain brings one to realization,
Of what is true and what is false.
What is lasting and what is not.

Tongue tip touched to palate…Allaah!
And deep dirt from the heart is scoured away
Polish applied, *AllahummasallialaMuhammed****
A shield to let in love that nourishes, not depletes
My heart is filling up, slowly, but it is a
                              permanent filling.

And slow permanency is better than a fleeting
joy

My Lord suffices me
And He is my Wakeel*

*Al Wakeel is one of the most beautiful names of the One Divine that means guardian, protector, shield, friend, refuge.

** makhraj means articulation point. The sounding of the One Divine's name 'Allah' is specific — the full curve of the front of the tongue must touch the upper palette to make the 'u' sound and 'l' sound which is then let out on a deep exhalation 'laH'. The 'al' is pronounced as one would 'um' in umbrella and not as 'ac' in accept.

*** Allahumma salli ala Muhammed means is 'O Allah, send your salutations upon Muhammed', it is termed the salawat, and is a means of remembrance.

∞

Al- Raqeeb*

Mercy descends in a voice that recites,
After a hard day's work into a long calm night.
Bathed in splendor of good,
lovingly looked upon

By a Most Beautiful Lord. Beauty with love adorned
Lulled into serene refreshed repose.
Tranquil in trust rest comes, gifted from the
One to one

Sleep brings a delightful glimpse of closeness.
Then refreshed, ready to greet another dawn.
Days so follow nights of the mu'min's** way in
this sojourn

Yet closeness to *Al-Raqeeb**
eases the separation.

*Al Raqeeb is one of the most beautiful names of the One Divine that means the one who is intimately near, closely watching over, the constant intimate caretaker.

** mu'min means believer

∞

Crescent moon new,
beneath it, Venus glowing white
like a star. Only more constant
Somehow.

And the setting sun casting
Shades of colour, through the atmosphere
in streaks, broad brush strokes,
That are clouds.

And lower yet, the naked silhouette
Of a plain May tree.
Shed of leaves and bare cones
Reach up to touch the sky.

Embracing it seems
Hands held high. Voice roaring in the
stillness of it all.

Both moon and star, cloud and tree
Exhibit their glory, to glorify Thee.

∞

Immaculate beauty

Behold caught upon my gloved finger,
And a moment before I did not see it.
Perfect in its gracefully tapering arms,
Perfect in its symmetry.
Stunning in its minute immaculate beauty.
A lone flake of snow. What a clumsy name,
For such a perfect union,
of the mother sciences,
And undiluted art.

This then holds the gift of life.
Miraculous molecule that births and sustains,
Every living form. Now a microscopic crystal
Then a mighty ocean, and then a wisp caught
on the air.
Then a rushing river, and then coursing in your
veins.
It is as if to say, how effortless for my Lord,
To create what is not only perfect art,
But also, perfect form.

Look! Look all around you, everywhere!
Millions of them my Lord drops,
Without a passing thought it seems,

Subhahanallahi wabihamdihi
Subhahanallah al-Adheem!*

∞

Love

A fall, in a split second
A fall that cut open a little's angel's face
My daughter. And my heart stopped
beating.

In a moment, to know
How deeply one loves. To recognize
This quality called 'wudd'*
It's depth, its encompassment, its
reaching
to the innermost core.

It takes pain to know love
It takes suffering to learn patience
It takes a shock to uncover
What God is made of.

*Al-Wadud**, The Love

To know that the human soul
is made of this thing called love.

*Wudd, means love. Al-Wadud is one of the
most beautiful names of the One Divine that
means The Love. That is, the fountain of love,
the source of love, the origin, essence and
completion of love in all, and for all time.*

∞

My rabb*

Your beauty dazzles, befuddles,
convolutes the mind
Mesmerised. This slave silently adores
Encrusted soul barnacles
Are scraped off painfully by pounding waves
Relentless. This slave weeps
Excruciating peeling away
Joyfully submitted under the roar
Cognizant. The slave is submitted
Grateful to be freed to receive
Light. Cannot be borne expect by
Polished heart.
Serene. Accepting this love pounding
That is unending. Only locked in a time space
vacuum
That is less than a moment in
semper-eternity
This slave loves.

Rabb means lord, beloved, guardian, owner.

∞

O' heart serene

I weep with yearning
To be with Thee. To return home
My heart yearns.

I weep anguished
Thinking what if. O what if my Lord
My heart's dirty

When that time comes
I miss the mark. So my heart cries
O' loving Lord,

Please don't deny me.
Let me be worthy when I return
My heart pleas

To stand before You
in purity. Iridescent, white.
I want to be

A heart of light

The reason being
Out of love. Because I love You
With all my love.

And so to please
The Beloved. I yearn for this
Pure return

To re-enter home
And say behold, O' greatest One
O' Perfection

I am home, happy
As long as you are happy with me
O' loving Lord

I pray overlook
and erase, my mountainous sins
O' Gracious Lord

O' *Al-Rahman*

For Thou art perfect
And my mightiest efforts summed
Equate to naught

Compared to Thy
Due. Yet this flawed creation
Is in love with

The Perfect Creator
And in that peace of knowing The Peace.
By Muhammed

I return to you
A heart serene, Made serene by Thee
Home joyfully

Al-Rahman is one of the most beautiful names of the One Divine that means the gracious tender love.

∞

Recitation

Teaching, guiding, soothing
Each morning before the sun rises
With the birds who wake before dawn
Learning their song. I recite
The revealed words of the Creator
As the earth stirs to life
So does my heart.
As cool gentle breezes of truth
Hum within my heartstrings
As the perspicuous light of guidance
Dissipates the doubt in my brain
As the wise and the true
Embellishes itself upon my heart
And then permeates into.
'O' Allah, mix it with my blood and
write it on my heart-muscle wall!'
I am but a grateful slave
of The One. One beyond time and place
One closer to me than my conscience.

One knowing me better than I do myself. So
then peace. In being in the safest hands. I am
gently led.
To a better way to live.

Each morning as I recite,
The words of my Lord. The birds sing. And
soon it will be dawn.

∞

The wind

Time has broken down.
And the memory that remains,
is in the wind-song.
Flowing through eons,
It touches my face.
And I remember the way I used to be,
Linking my past to my present to my future.
I know not where I'll be,
That sweet day the wind will,
Herald the long sleep, upon the way,
of my glad return.

∞

Al wadud*

Love I sought
    in absent lover's embrace
    in unresponsive friends
Love I sought
    from children who cling
    then grow and take wing
Love I sought
    inside of me
    but inside was empty

Then I looked up
    to the sky, beyond
    in despair, turned to where
My soul arose
    and there
    found the wellspring
Found
    the flow eternal
    flowing through me

I keep those valves open,
With my arms raised high,
And never yearn for love anymore.

But can give and giving,
Gain more.

From the One
*Al Wadud**, who made me
Who I came from

Allahumma razaqtani hubbaka**

** Al-Wadud is one of the most beautiful names of the One Divine that means The Love. That is, the fountain of love, the source of love, the origin, essence and completion of love in all, and for all time.*

*** this is a prayer that translates to — "O Allah, increase your provision upon me of Your love"*

∞

DU'A

Allah

O' my Lord, tell me,
How best to thank Thee?
Tell me how best I may please,
For in Thy pleasure does
my soul rejoice and
my heart find ease.

My Lord, true return
is only from Thee.
This, Your holy-word given
Manifold You return
And your promise is
Never broken.

You never sleep, nor
slumber. You are there
if I wake on a sudden
I am enveloped
By your loving light
Pain forbidden.

In the far reaches
of the earth, on
some alone hike, upward gaze
encounters the Divine
And I overawed
Adoring, dazed.

Stunned by your plenitudinous abundance.
Aware of my created-ness, my absolute dependence
Aware of your Creator-hood,
Your all-encompassing sustenance.

I say Your name over and over again
My will subdued, I am in worship
I call on You, to elevate me.

Heaven is beyond
Imagination
You have said. And also said
Paradise is here, in
snatches and glimpses
on this earth.

Look to the colours
of creation, then
The peace of the great rivers
The green of the trees and

great blue canopy
known universe.

Astounding beauty
Immaculate realm
Yet nothing it is, You teach
To the gardens beyond
the seven heavens
to Eden's reach.

And we were born to
They once in heaven
our parents Adam and Eve
(on them both be peace)
And so home calls me
I beg reprieve.

O' my Gracious Lord,
in the stillness of the ocean-depth
Myself at night alone with Thee.
Your beauteous countenance all about me,
My heart is stilled in awe, filled with great love
I say your name. And that is enough for me
Allah, Allah, Allah…

∞

Do not forsake me

How do I write
Of the deep peace I feel inside
Knowing the kindness of God
Illuminated for an instant
A nanosecond
Felt mercy
*Rahma**,
From *Al-Rahman**
Felt this, only after a day of striving
Overcoming, heart-ache, heart-break

I've lost my mother to a disease
Hugging her, into her vacant eyes my soul
looked
And felt the consciousness of God
To my knees humbled
When she thanked me
For teaching her to pray
To make *du'a***

*Allahumma, rabbi****
Without whom I am naught
I pray, do not forsake me.

**rahma, derived from the root word 'rahm'
meaning womb, means a nurturing merciful
tender love, such as that enveloping a fetus in
its mother's womb. A hallmark of the One
Divine's will upon creation, as the One
Divine has declared that 'my rahma
encompasses all things' (Quran 7:156)*

... وَرَحْمَتِي وَسِعَتْ كُلَّ شَيْءٍ

...wa rahmati wasiat kulla shaiyy
*Al-Rahman is one of the most beautiful
names of the One Divine meaning The
gracious tender love. It is derived from the
root word rahm.*
*** du'a means prayer*
**** Allahumma rabbi, means O Allah my
gracious beloved Lord, the One who looks
after and protects and upholds me.*

∞

Dhikr wa du'a al-farah

(remembrance and prayer of joy)

O Allah, show me the other side of reality
Teach me to live, make me grow
Nourish me.
Do not leave me alone
Even for an instant.

Help me to bear all the loss I know I must
Trusting it will be for the better
For returned to me will it be,
either better than it
Or my heart healed,
some unknown ill removed.

Help me. Put light upon light
In my veins, let light course,
In my eyes, let light shine.

In my lips, let light reside.
Off my tongue let light trip.
And flow on waves out to all around.

O Allah, I prostrate,
In complete adoration, I prostrate.
In complete joy, I am patient
Only because You give me patience
I fly
Only because You hold up my wings
Glory be to You, my most glorious Lord
Verily in remembrance of You,
Does my heart find peace.
*Allahumma anta Rabbi**
And I adore Thee.

*** *Allahumma anta rabbi, means O Allah,
you are my gracious beloved Lord, the One
who looks after and protects and upholds me.*

∞

Flight

Tufted clouds we pass over,
Up and down mildly turbulent.
Blue on white, streaks of light,
Radiate through striatal layers,
Filtering sunlight.

The Angel Meekail* has been at work,
And his work is majestic.
Beautiful artist, adorning continuous,
Works to please the Creator,
Glorification on high.

Puny I seated in this aeroplane,
With wings that don't know.
The mysteries of flapping flight,
So stiff outstretched we glide on.
The Mercy of the Lord.

Who but You upholds us?
A sudden jerk and my heart stops
Is this the time I meet the angel
One of that exalted race
Whose work outside I marvel at?

Or yet a few more years
One directional time, only growing less
Till my meeting. Longing then
To take my place as
The daughter of Adam.

And Hawwa**, Oh mother!
Of that Divine light,
That you and my father beheld
The traverse is long and hard
But the journey home is never too far
I am coming.

O Lord, guide me gently home
As you uphold the birds and guarantee
their provision
Keep me flying straight to you
My wings outstretched.

Hope and fear balanced
I do not deviate
My head a fountain of love
Forelock gently in your hand
I know my face is to the right direction.

Buffeted by the winds I may be,
But how can I fall?
When the Lord of Creation upholds me

∞

I make bold to worship you

You created Mothers my Lord,
Created their kindness,
                and the love in their eyes.
My soul fills with light knowing this.
Knowing Your love, You I adore, I glorify.

You created flowers my Lord,
Created their softness in soft heaps of petals.
Eye's delight in world coloured bright.
Seeing your beauty, You I praise, I magnify.

You created the wind my Lord,
Created its movement, that travels, fecundates.
Friend-wind that blows without ceasing.
Glimpsing your semper-eternity, I worship.

You created Fathers my Lord
Kindred kindness, human capacity to give.

My heart grows by your lavish grace
Feeling your cherishing-protection, I prostrate.

Knowing You my Lord,
        a bedazzled moment of closeness
A mesmerized moment of realization.
My heart is amazed and still.
My eyes water, my fingers tremble,
                          I am awed.

Terrified at Your greatness
Uplifted by Your goodness
Strengthened by Your compassion
I make bold to worship You My Lord.
     Subhahanaka Ya Rabb'ul'alameen!

     *a prayer that means Glory is Yours, O
     loving cherishing protecting Lord of all
     the worlds

∞

Making me

If you hadn't made me strong my Lord,
I would not have been able to resist.

If you hadn't made me just my Lord,
I would not have been able to stand-tall.

If you hadn't made me kind my Lord,
I would not have been patient.

If you leave me for a moment my Lord,
I will be destroyed.

∞

Purify

Purifying my gaze,
No, I do not mean not looking at that image
Of a half-naked woman on the billboard
I mean inside;

That when I stand in prayer,
I don't see the carpet,
But only that I stand before God.

That I don't see the mistakes,
of the *ibaad** next to me,
But only the angels on his either side.

That when I eat,
I don't see the food that waters my mouth,
But the *baraka** of *rizq**, and my neighbour,
Who needs me to share it.

That when I teach,
I don't see the rapt attention
of my student's face

Swelling my pride.
But I see the deep truth of what I talk about,
And I am in *sujood**, inside

So I pray,
Purify my gaze,
And the *hijab** on my head is simple.
Sometimes it is nothing at all,
But a head bent low.

Deeply ashamed of my weakness,
Deeply grateful for Your grace,
And I walk this earth in modesty**.
Purifying my gaze.

> **the meanings of the Arabic words are given
> below in alphabetical order:*
>> *baraka is blessing*
>> *hijab is veil*
>> *ibaad is worshipper*
>> *rizq is provision*
>> *sujood is prostration, it is the act
>> performed during the ritual worship
>> (vide pagina 41)*

*** the crux of the veil is that it is a symbol of modesty, which the One Divine enjoins on men and women. The mark of modesty being a gaze that is modest. As the One Divine instructs;*

> *Tell believing men to lower their gaze and to protect their chastity, that is purer for them...*
>
> *And tell the believing women to lower their gaze and to protect their chastity...*
>
> *(Quran 24:31, and 24:32)*

قُل لِّلْمُؤْمِنِينَ يَغُضُّوا مِنْ أَبْصَارِهِمْ وَيَحْفَظُوا فُرُوجَهُمْ ۚ ذَٰلِكَ أَزْكَىٰ لَهُمْ...

وَقُل لِّلْمُؤْمِنَاتِ يَغْضُضْنَ مِنْ أَبْصَارِهِنَّ وَيَحْفَظْنَ فُرُوجَهُنَّ...

> *qul lilmu'mineena ya'udoo min absaarihim wa yahfadhu furujahum, dhalika azkaa lahum...*
>
> *wa qul lilmu'minaathi ya'ududna min absaarihinna wa yahfadhunna furujahunna...*

∞

Safety

The mind threatens to raise its ugly head.
A forelock not grasped,
     in the hand of the All-Knowing.
Is liable to mighty error and deviance.

I have tasted the woes of this often,
And now abjure myself;
     'O self, would you lead me to hell
      When I may enter heaven?!'

So I abandon myself with glad abandon
And find safety in the refuge of my Lord
Who loves to be sought,
     And I love to seek Him.

My abilities exposed for their true state.
Not a synapse connects,
     except by the will of my Lord.

I am nothing and my Lord everything.
All I can be, and do, are empty mirages.

And all that is, is the One.
Who I beseech;
'O my Lord, do not leave me alone with myself
even for an instant,
Lest I, myself, destroy"

∞

Tasbih

The angels are writing
Every mouthed *tasbih, tahleel, takbeer**
Ah, the *tasbih* fills the scales from earth to sky
The angels are writing
Fervently writing. Kind, honorable
Noble scribes. On your right side
Know the angel is writing
And on your left, know the angel is smiling
His pen held high,
Subhahanallahi wabihamdihi
> *Subhahanallahi al-adheem***
Fills the space from earth to sky

*tasbih, tahleel, takbeer means to make glorification of the One Divine, to witness that there is no other worthy of worship except the One Divine, and to magnify the One Divine. This is done by invoking the phrases 'subhahanallah – glory be to Allah', 'la ilaha illa Allah –

there is no god but Allah' and 'Allahu akber – Allah is greater'. Were the veils to be lifted, it would be seen that all of creation is in a constant state of glorifying the One Divine, as the One Divine has stated, and some have witnessed.

> *All in the heavens and in the earth are in glorification of Allah, The Sovereign, The Pure, The Noble, The Wise (Quran 62:1)*
>
> يُسَبِّحُ لِلَّهِ مَا فِي السَّمَاوَاتِ وَمَا فِي الْأَرْضِ الْمَلِكِ الْقُدُّوسِ الْعَزِيزِ الْحَكِيمِ
>
> *yusabbihu lillahi wa fi-ssamawathi wa ma fi-lardhil-malikil-quddusil-a'zeezil-hakeem.*

***this formula means 'Glory be to One Divine and to the One Divine all praise and thanks, glory be to the One Divine, the Exalted, Glorious.' it is a formula of remembrance whose weight in the unseen dimensions is immense.*

∞

A thousand gestures of help through the day.
Have been strewn around me.
As I feel the angels on my shoulders
When I pause to greet them
*asSalamu alaikum**
asSalamu alaikum.

Not hastily uttered these words
Lest more blessing lost.
O Lord, preserve this slave in surrender
Humility guards
the heart's peace and mind's clarity.

The soul's joy is awareness
of every moment's miraculousness
This for the slave cognizant of God's bounty.

**Assalamu alaikum — The Peace be with you*

∞